T0128901

ON THE 28TH DAY, MY EYES OPENED

MICHAEL SANDERSON

ON THE 28TH DAY, MY EYES OPENED

iUniverse books may be ordered through booksellers or by contacting:

iUniverse
1663 Liberty Drive
Bloomington, IN 47403
www.iuniverse.com
1-800-Authors (1-800-288-4677)

ISBN: 978-1-5320-3919-5 (sc)
ISBN: 978-1-5320-3920-1 (e)

Library of Congress Control Number: 2017918784

Print information available on the last page.

iUniverse rev. date: 12/19/2017

INTRODUCTION

Before I start, let me introduce myself. I am Michael Sanderson, a 34-year-old African American male. I'm writing this because I have so many things that I would like to share with you about myself. Some are good, some bad and some just plain ignorant. You may form your own opinion about which is which. Feel free to do so.

DEDICATION

I dedicate this book to my Lord and Savior, who has made it possible for me to be here and to tell my story.

CONTENTS

CHAPTER ONE

WHEN MY EYES OPENED

When I opened my eyes, I just knew something wasn't right. Something bad had just happened, something really bad. I'm lying face up in a hospital bed. Metal is inserted into both sides of my neck to keep my head intact. A metal halo that kept my head in position had dug deep into my skin in my lower back, making my flesh raw meat.

I'm bandaged up like a mummy, hooked up to a massive machine that my life depends on, and have enough needles going into my body as if I were a human pin cushion. I'm motionless, helpless.

Three nurses are in the room diligently doing their duties in the process of repairing my beaten-up and bruised body. Family members and my on-again, off-again ex-girlfriend are seated around the bed right there in my face, overjoyed with love. I'm just waiting on somebody to tell me what's really going on.

I had a million questions but they were all tight-lipped about the details. All they told me was that I was in a bad accident in my truck. The only thing I was concerned with at the time, however, was whether or not I hurt anyone else.

"No, everybody was ok," I was told. "It was just a couple cars messed up but everybody was ok."

Somehow, I felt relieved. Even though I'm stretched out on this hospital bed, knowing that I didn't seriously hurt anybody else took the weight of a ton of bricks off my chest. Waking up just seconds away from death was not good either, but one thing was good about the situation—me just being able to wake up. It was such a good feeling to still be alive. Just 28 days prior, I had been in a horrendous wreck that nearly took my life.

Doctors and nurses said that most people couldn't have survived what I overcame. Chiropractors couldn't believe their eyes. Church members said that my miraculous recovery was nothing short of God's work. Some folks say that I had cheated death and won. I was just happy to be breathing.

The whole 28 days I was out of it, I don't remember a thing. When we leave this world, I wonder, would we even know we are gone? As far as heaven or hell goes, I believe it's really all about how you were living your life.

I say that to say this: do you believe in spirits? Well, I do and I'm going to tell you why. While I was asleep not even knowing if I were in this world or not, I asked myself over and over again if I wouldn't have made it through this, *where would I be right now?* I could be wrong, but who's to say? There's only one person who knows for real. If you were a good human on his earth, church-going, praising God's name, just being a good person, I think your spirit will inject into a pregnancy.

You can go to church seven day a week. You can be the best person in the world but if you don't know and have a relationship with JESUS, you will not make it into heaven. See, the word of God tells us in Romans 10:9-10.

"For if you confess with your mouth that Jesus is Lord and believe in your heart that God raised Him for the dead, you will be saved. For it is by believing in your heart that you are made right with God, and it is by confessing with your mouth that you are saved."

The Scriptures tell us "Anyone who believes in Jesus will not be disappointed." So this tells me it's just one way to get in to Heaven and that's though Our Lord JESUS Christ.

As far as heaven or hell goes, if you were good, your goodness will continue though another good human and if you lived the rough life—staying in jail, selling drugs, just bad by choice—then, your badness will continue through another bad human pregnancy. I could be wrong. I'm just going off of thoughts and feelings now.

It's not like you would remember when you're born and old enough to talk you're going to tell people, "I remember my old life. I had lots of fun."

You won't be able to say that because you would have all new insides and brand new brain. You would just be starting all over again. As far as my life goes, all I knew was that I was living my dream before my life was phenomenally spared from this tragic accident.

· · · · · ● ● ● ● ● ● ○○○○○○○○○ ○ ○

Since I was a youngster, I always pictured myself behind the massive wheel of a big work truck. When I grew up into a man, I was the one in control of this steel giant. And the very thing I loved for as long as I could remember nearly took my life.

According to the police report, I ran a red light. I honestly don't remember whether I did or did not run the red light. But that is totally out of my character. I don't remember the accident at all but, if I would've hit those cars head on, the impact would have surely killed them all.

Everything happened too fast. I was instantly knocked out cold from the impact of my battered body being thrown across the cabin like a lifeless ragdoll. When the tumbling finally stopped, I was turned upside down with all of my weight resting on my head. I admit I didn't have my seatbelt on but the doctors told me that if I would have been wearing one, it could have surely strangled the life out of me.

When the rescuers cut me out of the truck, they didn't know what was wrong with me. I had a huge bruise in the center of my forehead and burns all over from the muffler being hurled through the passenger side window.

By the time the ambulance rushed me to Huntsville Hospital, I was swollen up nearly twice my size. It took about a week before the swelling went completely down. Initially, doctors thought it was from that bruise but it wasn't. My condition was something much worse.

The doctor on call was a neurosurgeon by the name of John Johnson. It was only by God's blessing that neurosurgeon Dr. John Johnson was there. He checked me out and went out to talk to my family.

"This boy has hurt himself pretty badly," he told them. "You might need to make funeral arrangements. Statistics show that 97% of the people with this type of injury don't survive it.

"I am going to perform the surgery," he told them. "If all goes well, he will be paralyzed from neck down."

The medical term for my condition was *internal decapitation*. I broke my neck at a bone called C1. That's the bone that allows physical movement—talking, walking, eating. Without that bone, there is no you. In short, I had an internal decapitation of the neck.

Standing at 6 feet tall and tipping the scales at 330 pounds, I was a pretty big guy. Only my neck muscles kept my head from popping off my body. If I had been a small guy with a scrawny little neck, my head would have flown off my neck like a cork from a champagne bottle.

Doctors couldn't tell what was wrong with me because I was so swollen when I was first rushed in. They didn't want to move me around too much. They pumped me full of drugs to help the swelling go down before they could check me out.

They had to do three MRIs before they found out that my head was pretty much detached from my body. I went into surgery later that evening. It was only through the grace of God that I made it through. Only inches away from death, my family should have been making arrangements to put me in the ground.

After the surgery, the doctor came into the waiting room where my family was. He assured them that everything went fine in the operating room.

I was asleep for 28 whole days. I didn't even know that I was in this world. When my eyes opened, I looked like the Tin Man from the Wizard of Oz. I had so much metal attached to me that I resembled a robot. I was fused with titanium from C1 to C5. My head was being held onto my body with metal from my skull down to my upper back.

There was also a little piece of metal attached to the back of my lower skull. All this metal was attached as one. A halo was attached to me with four screws going into my head. It was used to support my head and actually keep my head on.

My family stayed by my side during those 28 days I was asleep. But to my surprise, my ex-girlfriend stayed there with me too. Even though we had recently split up, this woman never left my bedside. For the entire two-and-a-half months I was bedridden, she was right there. She had her mother take care of her children and made sure they got to school every morning.

Her mother stayed about 20 minutes from us and about 30minutes from the kids' school. She made it happen and I thank her so much for that.

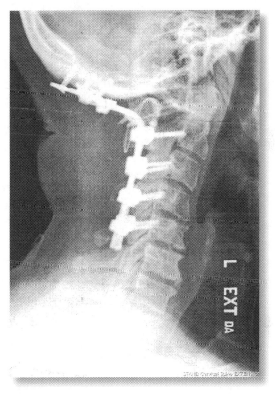

This is my x-ray, showing how my vertebrae were fused with titanium from C1 to C5 to hold my head onto my body

I engaged in countless conversations with my Heavenly Father for those 28 days I was in a coma. I think He was trying to decide whether or not I had been a good enough guy to remain living on His Earth. But while I lay there lifeless, I had a lot of prayers sent up for me.

One set of powerful prayers was from my next to older sister Sharon. She is a devout believer, a real church-going lady. She prayed over me constantly and chased the demons out of me.

The practice of praying over one's body goes way back to older generations. The spirit of the Lord takes over and supersedes any medicines that the hospital may give you. Let the old folks tell it, if you're near death and get prayed over and your body begins to show reactions like coughing or moving, the demons are exiting the body. And that's what was happening with me when my sister was praying.

She put a prayer on my wall so when people came in and read it, that was a prayer for me. Every time someone entered the hospital room, that prayer was read- all day long. Thank God for that. Those powerful words of prayer praising Him kept His hands on me. I cannot send up enough glory. So again, THANK YOU GOD.

As the days passed and I remained unconscious, my family said that I had been doing a lot of moving around. Before, I just lay there still and lifeless. The do*ctors had predicted that I would be paralyzed from the neck down. But when my body began moving in my sleep, they had to rethink their earlier diagnosis. They really didn't know how to explain my body movements if I was supposed to be paralyzed forever.

• • • • • • • • • ● ○○○○○○○ ○ ○ ○

With time rolling by with me still lying in that hospital bed, the doctors and my family had to figure out what would be done about physical therapy when I woke up. They got in touch with a hospital in Birmingham that offered the type of therapy that I needed. I still had tubes in my mouth and was hooked up to all sorts of different machines. They were going to have to take the tubes out and put this thing in called a 'trach', which would serve as a replacement for the tubes because Birmingham wouldn't take me with the tubes still in.

Through the entire process, family members said that I was calling out for my nephew Dion, who was out playing golf at the time. He, his brother Corey and his daddy Clifford were golfing fanatics. In our seemingly strange family tree, Clifford is my uncle and brother-in-law. He's my daddy's brother, which makes him my uncle and my sister's husband which makes him my brother-in-law. My sister and I have different fathers. So there is no blood relation between the two of them.

They said I was calling his name so they called Dion on his cell phone and told him. He dropped his club, darted off the course and headed straight to the hospital. Golfing didn't mean a thing right then; he was there in minutes to accompany me on the ride to Birmingham to be checked into Trinity Hospital. I didn't wake up from my coma until I made it to Birmingham.

CHAPTER TWO

GROWING UP

With nothing but time on my hands, my body clinging to life, I couldn't help but reflect on the trials and tribulations that these 34 years have shown me while coming of age in Huntsville, Alabama.

As far back as I can remember, my mom always took care of and provided for my siblings and me. There would have been six of us in all. Willie Jr. and Tonya died as children. I don't remember either of them because I am the baby of the family. The four of us that remained lived with Momma in Butler Terrace, one of the local housing projects in our city.

We left Butler Terrace when I was two years old and moved into a trailer park. I was too young to remember but that's where my biological father shot my momma in her leg with a .22. Momma knew she had to get away from this man before he killed her, so we moved into our family house on Jeri Street. We stayed there for about two months and then moved to Lincoln Projects in 1977.

I was just three years old when we moved into Lincoln Projects. I started going to the Boy's Club when I turned six. It was a local hangout spot for boys aged six to 18. And we loved it. We had a lot of good times there. I couldn't wait to get out of school every day. The staff there was pretty cool too. They showed us how to shoot pool, play table games and schooled us every other sport imaginable. They helped us with our homework. And to top it all off, they even fed us. I think that may have been my favorite part.

While I was doing this on a daily basis, my sisters were busy doing other things. Two were mothers and Nay was hanging out at the skating rink, which I would learn to enjoy later. During this time, a lot of things were changing and happening. Some were good; some were bad. There used to be a corner store within walking distance of the projects called Al's Angels that we used to frequent.

There is always a corner store in the projects, even in the movies. And Lincoln Projects was nothing different. We would go there to get snacks or play the Pac Man game. Sometimes Al would let certain people get things on credit because he knew many of the families lived from paycheck to paycheck. He was a pretty cool dude. He looked out for us and we looked out for him as well.

Sadly, one of the guys from the hood felt a false sense of entitlement one evening and tried to rob Al. No one really knows what happened that day except the two people who were there. One is no longer living, so we can't ask him. The other is serving life in prison.

Despite all of the temptations surrounding us—drugs, crime, delinquency, gangs—I still managed to do something productive with my young life. I got a summer job at my most favorite place during my upbringing—you guessed it—at the Boy's Club.

Now, I was the one teaching the younger boys the things that were taught to me. And I was feeling good about myself. I was 15 and had managed to stay out of trouble, in school, and I was a working young man. Not only was I helping young boys but I was able to help Mom out at home with the extra money I was bringing in.

Mom had a job cleaning houses for the so-called rich people who lived about 25 minutes from the projects. They paid her around $35 a day. Back then, that was pretty decent money.

Around the time I was in my early teens, most of my three sisters had moved out. It was just Momma and me now. I had no complaints, though. We did just fine and got by with a little help from one of her friends.

Meanwhile, I was busy going to school, working at the Boys' Club and hanging out with my friends at Rainbow Skating Rink. That was the place to be on Saturday night. Everybody would be in their cliques. Everything was cool until somebody would get the big head and think they were tough. That's usually when the dust began to fly.

There was always somebody who thought they were tougher than somebody else. See, the thing about living in the projects is that you automatically had beef with the other projects and vice versa. So if two people beefing with each other were from two different projects, war had been officially declared between the two sides. Whatever cliques they were from, they'd go to get their boys. Sometimes the damage was crucial.

One time, my cousin was in one of these fights and was cut on his back with a razor. I guess he was so busy swinging that he didn't notice until he got back to the 'hood. It was serious enough that he had to go to the emergency room and get stitches. That boy was foolish. On his way back home from the emergency room, he saw the guy from the skating rink and started fighting him again. Those were the days.

In the interim, Momma is getting cozy with her new friend. They were getting real cozy. He was a pretty nice guy and just what Momma needed. He wasn't like the usual riff-raff that you would find lurking around the projects. He had a good job and lived well. He dated my mom for about five years and felt like she deserved better than the projects.

Now, don't get me wrong; we didn't feel like we were better than the projects. It's not where you live, but how you live. He just felt like she should have done better for herself and wanted more. There's nothing wrong with that. And besides, she indeed deserved better. She was hard-working and provided well for her children.

With her friend's help, we ended up leaving the 'hood and moving to a nice house in the suburbs. Unfortunately, I was no longer in school. I quit in the 12ᵗʰ grade because I wasn't going to have enough credits to graduate. So as time went on, I remained living well and working good. I kept a job.

In 1996, I worked as a janitor at Huntsville Hospital. I worked in environmental services for the hospital for two years and then switched to the linen department in 1998. After a year, a position came open for a truck driver in the linen department at a building in Madison, which was affiliated with all the hospitals in Huntsville, Athens, Decatur and Marshall County. This was my big break.

I had already known my true calling in life since I was a snotty-nosed little boy. And now was the time to answer it.

Ever since I was a kid I've always liked big trucks. I can remember being in the projects standing on the street trying to get the truck drivers to blow their horns as they drove through. I just loved the powerful sound of the horn, and still do to this day.

Finally at the age of 25, I landed a job as a truck driver for this company called Health Group of Alabama. I was responsible for delivering clean linen to all of the hospitals around Huntsville, Athens, Decatur and Florence.

Even though that was the name of the company, they were still affiliated with Huntsville Hospital. After two-and-a-half years with the company, my assignment ended. I got laid off and started drawing unemployment. During this time, I started driving dump trucks for a guy named Mr. Beacher. I stayed at that job for about a year and got bored.

Driving dump trucks was okay, but I wanted to drive 18 wheeler trucks.

So after figuring out the necessary steps I needed to make in order to pursue my dreams, I went to truck driving school for two weeks to get a CDL driver's license. I learned how to shift the 16 gears, steer, backup and all of the rules of the road. If you pass all your classes, you were guaranteed a job at the end of graduation. I passed on my first try taking the test and landed a job with Falcon Truck Driving Company. Here, they placed me with a trainer and we hauled rolled steel on a flat bed trailer, covering all the northern part of the country.

That was cool, but when you have a trainer that doesn't take care of personal hygiene, that's not good. Those trucks have two beds in them—one on top and one at the bottom, like bunk beds. So when one is driving, the other one is supposed catch up on some sleep. It's so hard to sleep, however, when you're dealing with body odor reeking from your driving companion.

Two weeks had passed on the road and I got a phone call from Alabama Concrete offering me a job. They offered great pay and a good benefits package. Getting paid every week, good benefits, paid vacation and holidays off sounded good, but what made it sound so much better is that I wasn't going to have to smell any more body odor. It didn't take a second thought before I took that job with Alabama Concrete.

I could really get used to getting up in the morning in my own bed, getting ready for work, going to work and going home at the end of the day. I was like a kid at Christmas Eve. I didn't know how to act. I'm at home driving a truck with only one person—me. Life is great! I have nothing to complain about.

Around this time, I'm living at A 224 Conley Drive in Toney, Alabama. My paternal grand momma owned a lot of the land on that street. Her living kids still live in that area. One evening I got off work and made it home. I'm relaxing with the family that I had back then. The phone rang while I was lying in the bed and it was my dad, who lived next door.

"Get up," he demanded. "I think something is wrong with your uncle."

This was his sister's husband; they lived next door to him. My aunt Irene worked 12-hour shifts from 6 in the morning until 6 at night at a CD factory called Cinram. My uncle was home alone. It was not looking good. He died in the door way.

We got in touch with my aunt at work as quickly as we could and told her she needed to come home because something bad had happened. Boy, was it rough. Her reaction wasn't good.

Less than a week later, Uncle was peacefully laid to rest. Tons of family and friends showed up to the funeral to pay their respects. He was put away very nicely. He wore a black suit and there was a seemingly endless array of flowers. My aunt held it together well. Little did we know, however, that would not be the last time death would come knocking.

CHAPTER THREE

FAMILY & FRIENDS:
GONE TOO SOON

My cousin Ralph Pruitt was in this motorcycle club called the Showtimers. He was a real good bike rider. He was always at my house because I used to have strippers over every now and then.

Ralph and his bike-riding buddies were over to his mama's house one night talking and having fun. Without warning, Ralph hopped on his bike and left without saying a word to anybody. As he made it to the end of Conley Drive, he took a left turn and headed down Mt. Lebanon Road flying at the speed of sound. All of a sudden, his bike shut off. His boys took off to see what was going on. When they made it to Ralph, it didn't look good.

They say that he was going about 120miles per hour. Somebody was backing out of a driveway and he had to suddenly hit his brakes and went flying up in the air, landing on his neck. My cousin was pronounced dead on the scene.

My cousin was laid to rest on May 5, 2006. People packed into Mallard Creek Primitive Baptist Church to pay their final respects to him. The church was so crowded that some people had to stand outside. Family and friends stood up and talked about good memories that they had with him. My dad got up and sang the old hymnal "I Won't Complain." The song was very touching for someone that's being put to rest. There were so many bikers there.

At the cemetery as he was being lowered into the ground, the bikers all fired up their bikes. After all the tears had dried up and everybody went back to living their lives, the memories still weighed heavily on everybody's hearts—even up to this day.

Days later when I'm back at work, I was trying to put together a song in Ralph's memory. If there was anything that I loved as much as trucks, it had to be music. I loved how music moved me and made me feel. Music had the ability to take me on an emotional rollercoaster within intervals of just a few minutes of sound and emotion. While I was out on that road driving trucks, music was always there.

So I felt it was only fitting that I dedicate a song to Ralph. He was my first cousin and we were close. The song was called "Nightshifts." With the accident happening to him at night, that was the time that the Lord was ready to call him home.

Only seven months had passed since my father delivered that moving song at his nephew's funeral when he began to get sick. He lived just next door to me. We took him to the hospital, where he remained under a physician's watchful eye for several days. Everybody in my family would go up there, sit with him and keep him company. One day I went up to check on him and he was doing very well. So I left to take care of some things.

Later that evening I got a call from his niece Emma, his sister's daughter. "Your daddy is about to come home and he said to go turn on the heaters for him because it's cool outside," Emma told me.

I made it home and went over to his house to turn on the heaters like I was asked. I was so happy that he was finally coming home. I got the place heated up and went back next door to my place. Time is still ticking and I'm saying to myself, "Where is daddy? He should be home by now."

My phone rings and it's my sister. She did not sound good. "What's wrong,?" I asked her. As I waited for a response, the seconds seemed like decades.

"Daddy's dead," she told me.

"I just got a call telling me to go turn his heaters on!," I demanded. "What happened?"

"Emma was bringing him home from the hospital," my sister cried. "He asked her to crack his window because he was hot. She cracked the window and asked if he felt better. His head dropped down and …"

Daddy was initially hospitalized because of stage four brain cancer. He had a heart attack on his way home. It was his 61st birthday.

My daddy, George Hardin, better known as "Big Stack" had gone home. I miss my father but I'm glad he went in peace.

People have been telling me for a long time that death comes in threes. Even though it has happened to me and I am now a strong believer, I still had to question does death really come in threes? Keep reading and you will see why I made that statement.

My uncle Rose passed along on April 4, 2005. Then, my first cousin Ralph died on May 5, 2006. And my daddy passed on December 5, 2006.

Everybody was put away very nicely. My daddy even had his favorite song sung over him, "I Won't Complain," sung by my sister's friend Mrs. Linda Hill. His nephew, Roy Williams Jr., sang a song that my daddy really loved as well called "Bye and Bye." I know Daddy has no reason to complain now because he's in God's hands.

Daddy was a good man in his own way. He would cook enough dinner on Sundays for anybody who wanted a plate. That's just how much he loved cooking.

And don't let me forget about drinking and gambling. Big Stack loved his dice. He had a shed out back where it all went down. He left his family and friends with nothing but a whole lot of good memories. We think about him all the time and will love and miss him for the rest of our lives. May he rest in peace.

• • • • • • • • • ● ○○○○○○○○ ○ ○ ○

Through all of this death, I'm still driving my big truck every day. When I'm not driving, I'm writing songs. One night when I was in the studio putting in some work, I got a little tired and was getting ready for bed. The news was on but the volume was turned down so I couldn't hear what happened.

It was another motorcycle accident and it had had claimed the life of another man in Madison, a little town not too far away. I turned the TV off and went to sleep because I had to work the next morning. I made it to work that morning and all the faces were so down.

"What's going on?," I say to myself. One of the drivers came up to me and said, "Did you hear about Dameon?"

"What about him?," I asked.

Dameon and I were close. We went to school together. He was always in my Lincoln Projects breeding grounds. He started working for Alabama Concrete too. Dameon's truck number was 982 and mine was 983. We were crazy about our trucks. We would always turn down opportunities to get new trucks just to keep ours alike.

The company we worked for had four plants: north plant, south plant, Madison plant and Hampton Cove plant.

Dameon worked out of the Madison plant. I worked out of the north plant. Driving for Alabama Concrete, you could easily wind up driving all across Alabama.

When they told me what had happened, my heart just didn't know how to take it. Dameon was on Old Madison Pike on his bike when he collided with another vehicle. His life was taken instantly. I was down and out for awhile because we had just talked a couple of days ago at his plant. And I'm burying another loved one.

After I returned to work and was finally able to maintain a clear conscience, I'm sitting in my truck. The work had slowed down and a song hit me. The rhythm was nice as it bounced around in my mental but I had to put the words to it. It took me no time at all.

The memories of my friends and family that I'll never see again inspired a rest in peace song. These lives had been taken too soon. Hence the title: "A Life Gone Too Soon."

The song was for everybody I lost, but especially for Dameon. I have plenty of songs recorded but the only one that's been released is my Christmas album "Love for the Holidays" which was released in November 2004. It did ok, but not what I was hoping. I just had to look at where I was from- Huntsville, Alabama- a place where there is no love for music. But just keeping it real to all the out-of-town artists, Alabama's definitely got the sounds for you.

So here I am, dealing with all of this death surrounding me. Maybe God was trying to tell me something. Maybe I wasn't living right. Maybe I needed a change. I was wild and loose. I hosted many strip shows at my place. And before I drove trucks, I used to manage a club called The Truck Club. My stepdad, James McCartney and his partner Willie Bradford owned the club. They'd have dancers there too and that's where my introduction to that night life all started.

After a while, I got tired of that lifestyle and wanted companionship. I was married before and that didn't work out because she loved the clubs too much. She had three kids that I was helping her raise. She didn't care about making our marriage work and not only that, I had to deal with baby daddy drama. But I took it for the end of the road that it was and moved on.

So I'm living alone and still waiting on love to enter my life. I'm at work one day and my ex-homeboy Mark called me up. His old lady was locked up so he said, "You want me to get my girl to hook you up with somebody up there?"

He continued, "She meets a lot of girls up there that's looking for a man."

"Man you think I'm into talking to somebody that's locked up? You crazy?," I asked him.

Then I thought about it. I said to myself that people change and whoever she is, I don't even know why she's locked up. After I slept on the idea overnight, I called him the next day and said, "Ok, what have I got to lose? She'll just be a friend for now," I told him.

He told his girl and she said that she had a friend up there named Shan that wanted to hook up with me. When I found out who it was, I remembered Shan from way back in my past. I met her years prior through a mutual friend Tony. I used to see her when I'd take Tony back and forth over to her house. Or Tony would call Shan to come pick her up every now and then. She was always looking good to me, but I never said anything to her.

This lady got my number and called. When I talked to her for the first time from jail, I told her that we could be friends. I couldn't wait to be her friend. She told me a little bit of what she had going on and I told her a little about me.

She was on work release and got out every morning to go to work. At the end of the day, she had to report back to jail. I would pick her up through the week when she got off. I couldn't take her in the morning because I had to work myself.

Sundays were like a free day for her. On Sundays, I was off so I'd pick her up at 8 a.m. and she would have to be back at 5 p.m. The worst part of my day was taking her back to that "ruff hole", as she called it.

When I got her back up there, we would still have a little time to talk before she went in. Now, I'm not going to lie, I'm starting to feel this woman and I have a big heart when it comes to loving. I would hug her and give her a kiss on the jaw before she got out the car and I'd sit there until she got in. This woman was getting close to me, and so fast. All I can say is that this woman knew her stuff and knew it well. She had me and probably still does to this day.

Months into friendship with this lady, I wanted to turn it up a notch. Sometimes she got off work early so I started bringing her to my place. As time moved on, my feelings moved right with it. And those were some good feelings too.

She was young but she knew how to handle her thing like an older woman that's got her mind right would. She would cook and clean without me even asking her to. Not saying that my place was dirty and I didn't cook, but those were things that she just loved to do.

Then, the loving, oh my goodness, is all I can say. Everything was all good because I never had a woman like this. As it got close to her release date, I was so happy. What I had to get together inside of me was how I wanted to handle this when she got out for good.

Was I ready for more baby daddy drama? I got to thinking; this woman is so strong she might not put me through what my previous girlfriends with children had done. "It's worth a try," I said to myself.

This woman had five kids and I was just so ready to meet them. I met them and they seemed to be good kids. The oldest was 10 and the youngest was four. She was home free on July 12. I picked her up and we went back to my place. My plans were not to move another woman straight in with me but after she spent a few nights, it ended up being her home.

I wasn't tripping because she was doing everything a woman was supposed to do under a roof. After she was there a couple of days, we ended up bringing the kids in. Now we were one big happy family. And I was loving every minute of it.

I'm still driving trucks, living good and watching the kids enjoying their mama because she was away from them almost a year. She was still able to see them whenever she was at work or got a Sunday pass, but there's nothing like being able to see, touch, and talk to a loved one when you felt like it.

While she was locked up, my sister put together a cruise and when that time came to ship off, Shan would be out. She ended up paying her own way with her tips she made at work. That let me know what kind of woman I was dealing with. She was very independent, but keep in mind that I am a pretty good man too. So if the time came that she needed anything, I was there for her.

CHAPTER FOUR

VACATIONING ON MY FIRST CRUISE

The cruise was in September and I couldn't wait. This would be my first time flying and my first time on a cruise and I enjoyed the both of them. Everything seemed perfect. The downside was that the relationship had begun to lose its luster. I really didn't know anything about her past, but I think a little of it was starting to show at this point.

Some problems were caused by me and some by her. I know I'm not perfect and never claimed to be. But I dealt with the ends and outs for as long as I could. I was at work one day and got to thinking what I needed to do about this situation. I came home and asked her if she wanted to stay here and rent the place while I lived next door in my daddy's house.

Shan would have to pay rent to my nephew because I had planned to remodel my dad's place anyway. Nobody had been in that house since he passed away. She said that was fine. So I went to work, buying equipment and reconstructing the place. By the time I was done, I had spent $4,500 in the place. I still stayed there with her and the kids until I got done, hoping things got better between us. I still loved her, but from a distance.

I tried my best to stay focused on my daddy's place but it was hard being around someone that you love and don't know if it's going to work out. Sitting back watching the kids, even though I wasn't there when she gave birth to them, I loved them so much that I felt like I was there in the delivery room. Hopefully, one day everything would be like it was when I first met her and I hoped it would stay that way forever. She's a good girl, and her and those kids will always have my heart until the Lord sends for me.

We're out shopping and getting the stuff that we needed for the cruise because the time to shove off was getting close. Now, even though this lady and I have agreed to split up and live separately, we are still living together for now. I was just hoping that on this cruise, she wasn't going to treat me like she didn't know me. From the airplane to the boat, she had me feeling like she was still all mine. I thank God for the feelings that she was putting out to me because boy, they sure felt good.

When that magical morning arrived, we were all packed and ready to go. My sister and her husband drove us to the airport. It was still dark outside as we were on the road headed to our destination. We left that Friday morning and finally made it to the airport. As we got unloaded, my stomach began feeling kind of funny because it was getting so close to the time for us to get on this plane. Everybody just was sitting around talking, waiting on them to call for Miami, Florida. They finally did and we all piled onboard the plane, loaded up and were ready for takeoff.

The plane is rolling; it's rolling fast; it's rolling faster. Oh my goodness, it's lifting off the ground and we were airborne in no time. I had my eyes closed when we started going up but it wasn't so bad. I'm starting to like this. We had been up in the air for a while and I look down below. Everything was so small but I guess it would be when you're so far up. They just made an announcement that we were about to land in Miami.

The plane starts to ease down. I'm getting that feeling again in my belly. Things below are starting to look huge again. We are on the ground now, flying like a race car. We're slowing down, slowing down, and finally we are here. Everything went well.

We're waiting to be picked up and taken to the hotel where we will be staying until Saturday morning. We would be picked up again and taken to the cruise ship, and I couldn't wait.

When the day came for us to leave for the cruise, the van came to the hotel to pick us up and we were ready, too. We got loaded up and were on the road headed to the boat. My, my, my, we're here, man. What a big boat it is. If I'm counting right, it had nine floors. I guess you can say we were in a big building that floats on water.

We're about to head inside and give them our paperwork. They wanted to make sure that you were who you say you were before the boat took off.

So we're all ready to go up to our rooms. They have three different rooms. They have the regular one, which we were in. It was ok. We just had to push both beds together to make one but it was good for single people or people who were just friends. They had the rooms with the window in it so you could at least see the ocean as the boat is cruises.

Then, they had one with a balcony. You could go outside and sit down while the boat cruised. It also has a suite but I couldn't tell you about those because nobody I knew or has been with had ever been in one. But who's to say? Maybe one day we'll see.

As the ship takes off, we're unpacking now so we can tour the entire boat. We were only there for seven days but as big as that ship was, it was going to take the whole time just to tour it. That ship was just full of everything—casinos, live entertainment, swimming, games or you could just go up on the top deck and relax. It had plenty of areas to just lay back and take it easy. That boat had everything that you wanted to do, whatever you wanted to eat. And the best part of it all was that the food was free. Yes, I said free!

The first stop the ship made was a private island where they had food cooked for us and some games. They also had live entertainment and dancing. We stayed out there for a good while, until it was time to go back to the ship. They made sure everybody was back onboard on time so that we could take off and make our next port.

The next day was a day at sea. We stayed on the boat, still having lots of fun. The next morning, those that went to sleep woke up in San Juan, Puerto Rico. We unloaded everybody that wanted to go ashore. People who didn't want to go ashore stayed on the boat and enjoyed themselves. As we got off, they had so much stuff going on, little shopping outlets, food—good food too, but it wasn't free.

We had a good time. There was a lot of stuff to see. They had spots set up for drinking- plenty of ice cold beer, because boy, it was sure hot out there. They had mixed drinks too. We had a bus driver that took us all around the island, showing us many different places. One place that he showed us was this big drug dealer's house. At one time, this guy had the whole island on lock down. I think he's finished now, though. That was a long time ago. I don't have any idea what this guy is doing now. They didn't say.

As the sun was setting, it was time for the driver to take us back so we could load back up and set sail. I just went back to my spot at the casino, spending money, winning some and losing some. Most of all, I'm enjoying myself. We're back up in our cabin, getting some shut eye, wondering where we going to wake up to next. By the time we woke up, we're unloading again at St. Thomas, U.S. Virgin Islands.

We get on another bus. This guy's wife was a police chief. He drove us all around the island, showing us a lot of the little places. We made a couple of stops and he had us on top of this mountain. The view was lovely. You could see everything from up there. You could even see the cruise boat, beautiful.

Everything went great on that trip so we're back on the boat enjoying ourselves again. That night, they had something set up for those that wanted to participate. They had live entertainment set up.

As the days rolled by, I wondered where we were going to end up today because we only had a couple of days left to enjoy on this cruise. So they're announcing that the next stop would be the last stop before porting into the States. They drop you off where they pick you up. And I was not looking forward to that.

The final stop was at Grand Turk. Rather than tour the island, we spent the day at Jimmy Buffet's Margaritaville. What a nice place this was. If they were saving the best for last, they did a good job. This place had a live DJ, swimming, food, a lot of stuff to buy. I guess you can say we partied like it was 1999.

We had a good time. There was dancing and the DJ had it set up where you could win drinks because if not, you had to pay for them. I didn't want that day to end. But before I knew it, the fun was over and it was time to load back up on the boat. Goodbye, Margaritaville. I hope to see you again one day. And we are headed back to where we came from.

The next day, we would be on the boat all day, just having fun. So whatever it is that you had not done on this boat, you better do it because the next time you lay your head down to sleep, that will be your last time doing so other than on this boat. When you wake up, you will be awakening to exit, and it will be time to get back to regular life.

They had all kinds of stuff set up for us on our last night of the journey and we tried to partake in every offering we could until morning. When the sun came up the next day and it was time to say goodbye, the boat was jammed with hundreds of people getting off the boat. It was time to say goodbye to our tour and get back to driving trucks, raising my kids and making my music.

We unloaded and got back on the van headed to the airport so we could fly back to Huntsville. We're at the airport unloading and I was not even worried about the flight this time around. I was really looking forward to it. We are in the air now, talking about getting back to work. Our vacation was over as they announced over the air that we are about to land in Huntsville. I sure wasn't ready to hear that. I wanted to stay back in that fantasy land on the water.

Man, I wish that boat was here with us but there's nowhere near enough water for that boat where I'm from. Oh well, there's nothing wrong with wishing. We loaded up in the ride and headed home. If every vacation could go like this one went, I would love them all. My girl and I were back home now at 224 A Conley Drive ready to unload, get in the house, unpack and get our kids. I can't wait.

CHAPTER FIVE

BACK AT WORK, HEADING INTO MY ACCIDENT

Shan is a wonderful person but before we went on the cruise, we split up. We still went on the cruise together because it had already been paid for. On that ship, no one could even tell that we were not a couple and that was good. We really enjoyed ourselves. When it came time to eat, sleep, gamble, watch events, play games, we did it together. The plan was when we got back, she was going to live in our old place and I was going to move into my daddy's place next door.

I was remodeling before we left to go on the cruise. I guess I had spent about $4,500 so far and wasn't done spending yet. When we got back, I was going to finish. We unpacked and went to pick up our babies. Every woman I've ever dealt with has already had kids but that was not a problem to me because I love kids. I have seen how some women want to go to the clubs and get so mad because they can't find a babysitter. The kids didn't ask to be here; they were made.

I don't have any biological children, but the ones that I'm raising now are my kids. I never had to deal with baby daddy drama in this relationship. I had to deal with some crazy ex-boyfriends in past situations. The daddies would want to act up because a real man is there taking of his kids but I fault the woman as well, especially when they don't stand up for themselves. I'm so glad that's over.

But here's the thing far as the kids go, I love them all and it doesn't mater if me and the mama are together or not, that love doesn't have anything to do with her. I love all of them unconditionally. They always call me Daddy or step daddy when ever they see me so, I must be doing something right. Even though I don't have any kids of my own, that doesn't mean I don't know how to be a daddy. Plus, I have a lot of nieces and nephews so I've been trained very well when it comes to kids. Even though this lady and I are not going to be together anymore, it wasn't because of the kids we didn't make it as a couple so, the love still remains.

Tuesday morning back at work, I was bragging to all my co-workers about the cruise. I'm telling them all how they need to take a vacation like that before they leave this world and not even knowing that *my* almost leaving this world was right around the corner. I'm not wishing bad luck on anybody, but you just never know when the Lord will call for you.

After I got off, I went home and started back working on my place. Dark was about to fall so I would go back to my old place, which was just next door. I would take a shower, eat and then get in bed because I had to work in the morning.

Even though my ex-girlfriend and I are not together, you really still could not tell because I would still do stuff for her.

I would talk nice to her; we still slept together even though no sex was going on. I could still hold her at night when we got into bed.

• • • • • • • • ● ○○○○○○○○○○

It's Wednesday morning, September 19, 2007. It started out much like any ordinary day. I woke before the crack of dawn, crawled out of bed and got ready for work. I brushed my teeth and washed my face like I did every morning. I put on my pants and my shirt. Then I grabbed my keys and woke old girl up. I told her I was about to leave. She even walked me to the door.

"Have a good day at work and I'll see you when you get home," she told me as I headed out; I told her, "see you, too." That was nothing but love.

I headed in to the plant about 20 minutes early to service my machine and pick up my first load of cement for the day. Little did I know, it would be my last. I'm about to clock in and get in my truck. I got my hood raised checking my fluids, making sure all my levels are right, checking my tires making sure I didn't have a flat and none of them were low. Everything's good. I'm getting in line and waiting on a load.

"983, go East," said the loader man over the truck radio.

I got my ticket and headed to the wash rack to check my concrete and make sure it's like the ticket says. For instance, your ticket will have a word that will say "slump", and that will determine how wet or how dry the concrete was.

My ticket said "6-inch slump", where the concrete is kind of soupy; 4-inch slump means that it would be kind of stiff and sometimes it might call for fiber. If so, that will be up on the rack in some bags. I got my load together and I'm heading out to the job. My plant is on Springfield Road so I'm headed down it to Pulaski Pike. I take a left onto Pulaski Pike until I get to Winchester Road. I take a right on Winchester Road. And this is where it all goes down from what I've been told.

I head out the gate and as I'm beating down the highway sitting high up in the clouds, I notice a two-car fender bender up the road ahead of me. I veer to the left to avoid the accident. Because my trailer was fully loaded with more than 34,000 pounds of cement, my truck swerved so hard that the extra weight shifted the rest of the vehicle and flipped me completely over. The truck landed on its right side. The impact of the crash packed so much force that it tore the top vertebra from the base of my skull.

I was rushed to Huntsville Hospital and stayed in a coma for 28 days. Family and friends told me that I woke up in Huntsville hospital but I don't remember any of that. They told me I was moving around and my eyes were open; they would tell me to squeeze their hand if I knew who was talking to me, and I did; but the only thing I can say about that is, that was God giving my family and friends some sort of relief.

Just imagine if I would have lain there the entire 28 days without moving or responding in any kind of way. Some may have somehow given up hope.

I had a lot of doctors coming in and out checking on me. I was in the intensive care unit of Huntsville Hospital for three weeks before I was taken to Trinity Medical Center in Birmingham, Alabama. Trinity is a specialty hospital that provides care for those who need a level of care that's between intensive care and regular patient care. After three weeks there, I was taken to Spain Rehabilitation Center at the University of Alabama Birmingham Medical System. There, they helped me with physical therapy and learning how to eat right again. When you've been fed through a tube feed for almost a month, you have to get back used to solid foods. I did with the help of those sweet nurses and my family.

My primary care doctor was Dr. Pitts. He was there at Trinity Hospital too but I had about six or seven different doctors over there as well. When I got to UAB Hospital,

Pitts was there too but he was the only one that I had to deal with. Every time he came, he made sure I was doing well but the one thing that kept getting to him was the cut that they put on me to do my surgery. That was also where they had to go in and fuse me with metal.

"I don't like that," he said everyday he came to see me. "I don't like that," he just kept saying.

This is what my truck looked like after the accident

My cut was looking infected to him, because it was not healing right. The infection turned out to be a staph infection. Whenever he came by to check on me, it had pus running out of it. It was always moist. The last time it didn't look right to him, he got in touch with this neurosurgeon by the name of Dr. Pritchard. He came to see me and it did not look good to him either.

Another view of the truck taken at the accident scene

Now, I'm about to have another surgery. He's going to take out all my staples, open up my cut again, go in and clean out all the infection and staple me back up. I sure didn't like that. While performing this surgery, Dr. Pritchard found small fragments of bone and metal, which he removed along with the staph infection.

The good thing was that he did not have to go all the way down to the metal, but the bad thing was that my cut had to be opened up again. I pretty much had a double surgery. That was no fun at all.

My body had become so addicted to pain medicine that when I received medicine to put me to sleep, it didn't keep me asleep very long. I woke up just as they finished. That wasn't fair because I didn't get to sleep any of my pain off; I woke up when the pain was just getting started.

After that little surgery went down, I was looking at about a week to a week and a half before I could get out of the hospital and be at home with my family. I sure couldn't wait for that. So in the meanwhile, I remained, still going to therapy every morning, eating right, and just waiting on my release date. It was like I was locked up in jail but I'm just in a hospital.

I'm just taking it day by day. Shan is still by my side. It doesn't matter whatever happens in my life; I will love this woman forever. Everybody was taking turns coming up there to see me. Even though they still had to work, they managed to come see me and that's love. Driving one hour and fifteen minutes away from home, Huntsville to Birmingham just to see me, I feel so special.

My eating habits had gotten a little better to where my friend and I were walking down to the cafeteria to get something to eat. I wasn't waiting on that diet stuff anymore but it wasn't that bad, though. The therapy people were still doing their job and a good job I must say. They had this one lady whose name was Mrs. Sophia; she had these mind games set up for me to see if my brain was ok and it was. I did pretty well.

They say that when you have a major head surgery, sometimes it will mess with your brain. I really don't remember what happened in my accident because my Father upstairs put me to sleep before it happened so I wouldn't remember or feel pain. Thank you, Lord.

My days at the hospital are about to come to a close. I will soon be at home but when I get there, a nurse will still have to come out to check on me and make sure everything's going ok. They had to monitor my blood pressure and temperature for a couple of more weeks.

I'm still wearing the halo and I had to keep that on until December. I got released about a week and a half before Thanksgiving. It was the best Thanksgiving Day ever. We enjoyed that day out to my mother's house. We were already staying there, so I didn't have to get up and go anywhere. I remember staying at my mother's place until I got good enough to go home.

I can still remember waking up taking my medicine and setting the table to eat breakfast on Thanksgiving morning. I was so quiet. "Son, what's wrong?," my mom asked.

My head just dropped down. "I'm just thinking about the way I am now," I said to her, tears rolling down my face. "I was just thinking about the way I am now is the way I will be for the rest of my life."

I had pretty much no neck movement all the way around. I am fused in my neck with metal that's never coming out.

Just not being able to be like I used to be was causing me to have my breaking moments.

"God does things for a reason," she said to me. These words will be with me for the rest of my life. "There's a reason why you went through what you did. There's a reason why he kept you here."

I finally got myself together. The tearful moments stopped, but the thoughts were still riding my brain.

Thanksgiving is over and we're headed into December, the month that the halo comes off and I'll be glad when it's off because it's really hard riding in a car. You don't want to be out in public wearing one because it draws attention. So I pretty much stayed in the house and watched TV. I didn't even feel like writing songs. That was a major shock to people because everybody that knows me, knows that music and driving trucks is really all I'm about.

CHAPTER SIX

WRITING ABOUT MY ACCIDENT: MUSIC & BOOK

Before my accident, I wrote this song called "On My Way to Heaven." Ever since I've been writing, over 13 years, all of my songs have had three verses. You might get a song with two verses. But if so, the chorus to the song would be long. My song before the accident only had two verses and when I was able to go back in my studio, I played that song. While I was listening and I got to thinking about the 28 days I was asleep. I believe that's where I was on my way to. The third verse just came out of my head with no problem.

In the first two verses of the song, I'm on my way to heaven because that's where I was headed. When I got up to the gates, my Heavenly Father turned me back around because he still had work for me to do. Now that I'm back, I believe he wants me to get my story out to all of the nonbelievers who do not believe in Him. If there was not a God, then I would not be here to show and tell people what I went through.

I also wrote a song about my accident titled "28 Days." This song was written to let everybody know what I went through. I titled it "28 Days" because that's when I knew I was in this world again. Then came this song called "This Feeling." When that halo came off, the feeling that I was dealing with had me tired of living. So this song was written in the midst of that.

Then, the last song out of the four new ones I wrote is my favorite, "God's Blessings." In this song, I thank God for blessing me with a new life and my same talent he's always blessed me with, being a pretty good writer and if you're reading this book right now, these are the songs that come with my book: "On My Way to Heaven," "28 Days," "This Feeling" and God's Blessing." Now the last song with my book is also one of my favorites, "I LOVE YOU MAMA", yes, GOD is my creator, but she is my creation. I hope you enjoy what you're reading and what you hear. Be BLESSED.

As the days pass and the countdown ends, it's time to get that halo off me. My new song "This Feeling" exemplifies my emotions during this time. I was kind of worried about how it was going to feel, because they had to unscrew the four screws that were holding my head on.

The man that I've been calling Daddy since I was 13 years old took me back to Birmingham to have the halo taken off. The doctor who did my second surgery had one of his guys take it off. I had to sign in when I got there and wait to be called to the back.

"Michael Sanderson," the nurse announced, poking her head through the door.

"Yeah, that's me," I said.

I was so ready for this thing to come off. We headed back to one of the rooms in the office. He got his tools- as if he were changing oil or installing a transmission. He had to unscrew the screws that were holding the halo in position. And I'll tell you this: it was not a good feeling.

My skin and hair had grown in and connected with the screws. As he twisted and turned, my skin snapped off. My hair was being pulled from the roots—not a good feeling! When he was done twisting as far as he could, he had to pull it apart.

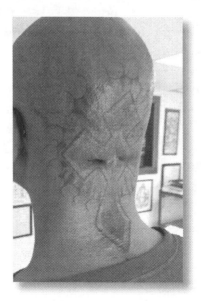

These picture show the length of my surgery incision, from the middle of my head to the base of my neck.

"When this thing comes off," he says, wrestling with the contraption, "I will have to give you a neck brace because the halo will not be there anymore to support your head. We'll have to get you some therapy set up."

The halo came on off and man, did it hurt. Now, instead of this circular steel apparatus doing all of the work holding my head in place, my muscles will have to do their job. I may have been in pain, but it sure felt good being able to sit normally in a car again. Thank God.

I'm still having doctor's appointments in Birmingham and I always will until Dr. Pitts and Dr. Pritchard release me. But it felt so good to be back home without that halo. Even though Shan and the children were still at my house, I wanted to be with my mother. After all that I had gone through and was still going through, I needed Momma around. Nothing against Shan. She's a beautiful person.

An added bonus to the halo coming off was that my favorite time of year is about to arrive. Christmas is right around the corner and we will celebrate it at my sister Doris' house; we call her Ann, a lot of people do. We had a good time, at least I did, being there without that halo. It was so nice.

When the holidays ended and I'm getting ready for therapy, it's time for me to move back in my place—with my family. We told Momma thanks for everything and now I'm well enough to be at home. We got everything packed up and we're on our way home to get things back in order because we hadn't lived there in almost four months.

We left Momma's house at the end of December and brought in the New Year at home. As we waited on therapy to be set up, the family and I just laid low at the house. Yes, my friend and I are back together now and it sure feels good saying that again. I just hope it lasts.

I got a call from my case manager and he said I would be going to therapy three times a week at a place across from Huntsville Hospital. I called and got it set up. Everything went fine in my appointments; the only thing was that I was full of conversation. I wanted to know what good exercises were going to be, as far as the tightness in my neck. They told me it will help me get strength back up because while I was laying in the bed for a month straight, I lost a lot of my strengths. That went on for a couple of months and then I had to go back to my doctor in Birmingham and he would determine if I needed more therapy or not.

"I want to set you up for some work hardening," D. Pitts told me after the session was over.

"Okay," I said, "What's that?"

"Well, it's like therapy but it's the therapy that gets you back in shape for work," he revealed.

I said okay because he's the doctor and I felt like he knew what he was doing; I hoped. I had to get in touch with a guy by the name of David, the therapist who was over the functional capacity evaluation test at the center where I was going. I did and now I'm back at the same place seeing the same people but just dealing with him.

Instead of going to therapy three days a week, now it's five days a week, four hours a day but that's cool. We walked every morning outside and exercised inside right after we were done walking. That went on for three weeks and after it was all over, I had to take a functional capacity evaluation test. That's a test that lets you know your strength level, to see how much you have built up since your first day.

After that was over, of course I had to go back to Birmingham to Dr. Pitts to see what he had to say this time. I'm with him again and he's checking me out and wanted me to go back to work for four hours a day.

"Doing what?," I asked. "Do you mean doing light duty work like cleaning up or something like that?"

"Driving," he answered.

He wanted me to get back in them big trucks again. I was shocked that he would send me back on the road with pretty much no neck movement. Now, he wasn't the only doctor I was seeing. I had to see Dr. Pritchard.

When I told him that Dr. Pitts wanted me to go back to driving, he asked, "Do you have to turn your neck left and right a lot?"

"That's the only way you can deal with a truck like that," I told him. "When you're on the job pouring out concrete, you have to watch the guys in the back of the truck and they're moving left to right."

I'd have to climb ladders, bend over and turn my neck constantly. With hardly any neck movement, going back to work was going to be hard for me.

Dr. Pritchard said that he didn't think it would be a good idea to drive. I said ok. Now it's only up to my job whether or not I should return to work. When my boss found out that I couldn't drive trucks any longer, he didn't like that at all. He told me I could drive his dump truck because it didn't leave the yard.

I called my employer and spoke to Ms. Cheryl, the lady who took care of all the truck drivers' needs regarding insurance, dental, 401K, and Workman's Comp. When I called to ask whether or not they wanted me to come in, she was shocked too but she said that she would get back with me and let me know something.

Some family members and I were going out of town for the weekend. We had an incredible time Friday through Sunday. That morning Sunday morning, I got up and checked my voicemail from the office manager at my job.

"Hey, Michael," she said. "We have some work for you to do, so be here Monday morning at 8. See you then. Bye."

"I wonder what it is," I thought to myself.

When Monday morning rolled around, I got out of bed at 6 a.m. and I'm trying to get up and get ready for work. I usually I eat breakfast in the morning before work but that morning I wasn't hungry because I was too worried about what I was going to be doing.

It's 7:30 and I'm headed to work. When I got there, everybody was so glad to see my face again. Boy, I tell you I felt like a star. But after I found out my daily tasks, I didn't feel like a star anymore. When have you ever seen a star cleaning up for people? I've went from driving a big truck to being a janitor. The one good thing about it was that they didn't touch my pay. I made the same wages I did as when I was driving trucks.

I worked four hours a day from 8 a.m. until noon for awhile. The only thing I did not like about that is while I was sweeping, I was sweeping up a lot of dust. And sometimes the drivers would be in my way. I didn't want to ask them to move because they had work to do too. I went and talked to the boss, I asked him could I start coming in a little early and just have everything done by the time they got there. He said that was fine. So I did that for a while then he wanted to have me tested to see if I could drive trucks again.

When my boss found out that I couldn't drive a truck any more, he didn't like that at all. He told me that I could drive this particular dump truck because it didn't leave the yard. It just went to the plant next door to get gravel and sand and bring it back and forth all day. He didn't really need anybody to clean up so it was either that dump truck or they didn't need me at all. Reluctantly, I took the job. I never got to drive the truck because I was being trained by another driver.

The first day I got in that truck, the boss man had his son cleaning up around the plant- even though he told me he didn't need anybody for that job. He wanted to keep it in the family; I guess. But all of the bumping and banging for just a couple of hours started to aggravate my injury.

While working, I'm still having doctors' appointments, so I'm back and forth in Birmingham visiting Dr. Pitts. On my first visit since I was back at work, the first thing that came out of his mouth was, "How is the driving going?"

"I couldn't tell you because I haven't been driving," I said.

"Why not?," he asked.

"They just don't feel like it's time to put me in a truck right now," I said.

"Ok, I tell you what. I will find a way to get you set up for some more therapy," he said. "And I'm going to have a guy come out and do an on-the-job analysis."

David was the same guy that I was doing this work hardening therapy with. He was to come out to my job and see exactly what I had to do as far as the lifting, driving and any neck movement I would have to use. Because I'm limited, he would be checking all this stuff out.

Now, two weeks of therapy are set up for me again and the time was going to be from 8 to 12 Monday thru Friday. I had to let my job know because I would be losing an hour and a half for two weeks. We got everything worked out in no time and I was back in therapy. Dr. Pitts had set me up to come back and see him one month later from my last visit and the analysis was done.

While I was still in therapy, I wanted to find out what was said, so I went and ask David myself. I said, "David do you think I will be able to drive trucks again?"

"Yeah, I think you can drive again," he said.

"But will it be safe?"

"No," he said, "I think you can drive anything you want but you are in a situation that you would have to think about your safety first."

"Well that's how I feel about it," I told him.

"Well, that's a decision that you would have to make," he said.

"You're right," I told him. "And I will."

Now all that's over with and it's time to go see Dr. Pitts again. My case manager is here as well at my doctor's appointment in Birmingham, just waiting on him to come in. He had all my paper work from therapy and the analysis to give to the doctor. Dr. Pitts came in, got the paper work and looked over it. He must not have liked what he'd seen because he left out the room for a minute and when he came back he asked, "What kind of license do you have?"

"Class A driver's license- a CDL," I told him.

"Is that what you need to drive that truck?," he asked me.

"No, you need Class B but with the ones I have, you can drive anything," I told him.

This doctor wanted me to go take another driving test that would also knock my Class A down to a Class B, meaning that if I wanted to drive an 18 wheeler, I couldn't—ever. He wanted me to let my job know because if I took another driving test, it would have to be through them. I would even have to use one of their trucks.

I made it to work the next morning and I told the office manager that Dr. Pitts wanted me to take another driving test. "Okay," said the office manager. "But first you will need to take a DOT physical because your old card has expired."

Now these are the doctors that you go to that will only let you drive if your body is in perfect shape. She called Occupational Health Group Medical Tower and set the appointment up for me and I went. I made it there, signed in and they called me to the back. I explained to the doctor what had happened to me and what I had to deal with for the rest of my life. "Son, I know you have already heard this before," he said looking at me seriously. "I'm just glad to see you here through this accident and I know you have heard this before. People don't usually make it through this."

"Yes sir," I said. "I have heard it a lot."

"I don't think it would safe for you to be out on that road in your condition," he said.

I said I agreed. "I cannot give you a card," he told me. "I'm sorry."

"Okay, thanks, doctor," I said.

"Without this card, you can't drive any commercial vehicles," he informed me.

The next day I'm back at work and I gave Miss Cheryl all my paper work from OHG. She faxed it to workmen's compensation. Now, Dr. Pitts wanted to see me again after I passed this test because he was going to set up some more work hardening for me. More therapy would get me stronger.

My case manager said, "Well, Dr. Pitts, if he passes this test ..."

"Hey! Stop. I don't want to hear that," Dr. Pitts interrupted. "I don't want to hear that, just say when he passes this test. Okay?"

My case manager said, "Okay, when he passes it, you want him to come back and see you, right?"

"Right," Dr. Pitts said.

Now, I really don't know how all of this is going to come out as far as this being a workmen's compensation case. I had to get an attorney. I decided not to use the first firm that I chose. They were all family but when I took him my hospital bills just from Huntsville, he said, "This is the biggest bill we ever had to deal with."

Just the Huntsville bill alone was $1.2million and that wasn't even including Birmingham's medical bills. Now the restrictions are permanent. No more driving big trucks and no lifting over 45 pounds. Right now, I'm still cleaning up for them, but they don't really need me there for that. I went to work one morning and Miss Cheryl told me that workmen's comp had called them and wanted to know if they had work for me to do. She told them that she would get back with them. She talked to the boss man and he said the only thing he had was driving a dump truck to get gravel and sand, that the position that I spoke about earlier.

That was the only position they had open. And if I didn't take it, I pretty much wouldn't have a job. I had to talk to my attorney to let him know what was going on. He said that he didn't think that was a good idea since I was restricted from driving big trucks, but he wanted to talk to some people first and would get back with me. I said okay.

CHAPTER SEVEN

DEALING WITH ATTORNEYS FOR MY CASE

About a week had passed and I hadn't heard anything from my attorney yet. I got to work one morning and the office manager told me that workmen's comp had called her and said they would be sending somebody down to give me this test that was going to determine, as far as my body goes, what I would be able to do.

A couple of hours later, the office manager called the workmen's compensation people back and said she talked to her boss. He told her to tell me not to worry about the test. I said okay, and called my attorney to tell him they called the test off. "Well, that sounds like total disability to me," he said. "Just let me know if they say something else."

My birthday was rolling around and I wanted to be off for it. I was off Saturday, Sunday and Monday, the day my birthday fell on, as well as Tuesday. When I got back to work on Wednesday morning, the office manager came in and said, "Hey, workmen's comp sent your attorney a letter and we need to know if you're going to take this job. So just get back with us as quick as you can."

"Will do," I told her.

Now the pressure is starting to get heavy. I talked to my attorney again and he said, "I talked to workmen's comp and what they want to give you, I just don't think that's enough.

He continued, "I think when this thing is all over with, you should have at least $150 to $200,000 but let me talk to some people because they're just trying to get off easy."

I said, ok again. But let me say this, I really didn't care about how much money they give me because none of that would ever equal up to what I got right now: my life. They had $45,000 on the table along with my job and my same benefits. They would just have to cut my pay. All of that sounded pretty good to me but my attorney was telling me a bit different.

"You just do what you feel like you need to do," he said, "because they're just trying to get over."

"If I don't take it, then who is going to pay my bills?" I asked.

"You're right and you've got to do what you got to do," he said. "Just call me in the morning and let me know what you decide."

People always assumed what I was going to get, but whatever I get it will be because of my Heavenly Father. I was running out of time. Everybody wanted to know my decision because if I showed back up in the morning, it would be to take that job. I'm thinking real hard but at the same time not letting it get me down. I went to work. It felt funny being there at 7:30 instead of 5 but when I got there, the boss said he would be with me shortly. So when he came back to me, he had their dump truck driver to show me what it is that I will be doing.

"I've got two questions for you," I told the boss. "I need to get off at 10:30 because I have an appointment. And could I still be off every Saturday like I was?"

"I don't know about that," he said, "because that would leave this guy here by himself."

I said okay because he was the boss. I got in that truck and it felt kind of funny because I was not supposed to be driving. He showed me what to do. All that bouncing around was not feeling good to me. I was glad I was only there for a couple of hours. Before I left, I told the office manager all that bouncing around did not feel good to my neck.

"You probably just have to get use to it," she said.

I left at 10:30 and I guess at about noon, I called her and told her that I was aching really badly. And I was about to take a muscle relaxer and lay down. "Okay," she said. "Call me and let me know how you're doing."

I had an appointment at this spine center to see if they could help me with some of the tension in my neck. When I got there, I took my X-rays with me from Birmingham so the doctor could see what was going on with me. All the paper work was filled out and I'm just waiting to be called to the back.

"Michael Sanderson," a voice called out.

I got up and went to the back and the nurse checked me out and my X-rays and said to me, "It's just a blessing that you're still here."

"I've heard that a lot," I said.

"The doctor will be with you shortly," she told me.

What led me down here was this television commercial I kept seeing. So I decided to check them out. I'm here now just waiting on the doctor. When he arrived, he shook my hand and told me his name. I told him mine.

"I saw your x-rays and I just want to say I'm glad to see you're still here today," he said. "After all of this and with what you got going on, we wouldn't be able to do anything for you because the way you are fused from your skull down to your C5 bone, we would hate to mess with that."

I left the doctor's office still aching from riding in that truck. I went home and put some heat on me, took a couple of pain pills and relaxed. That next morning at about 2 a.m., I woke up and took another pill because I was still hurting. I didn't wake up on time so my friend Shan called in to work for me.

When I woke up, I called in and told Miss Cheryl that I was aching too badly to come to work and I might be in the next morning if I'm feeling better. I laid around all day and got myself feeling a little better. I went in the next morning because I felt a little better. I was back in the truck again, still not driving though.

I bounced around in that dump truck for a couple of hours and had to go see about a doctor. Miss Cheryl said, "If you want to see a doctor you would have to go see Dr. Pitts." That's my care doctor in Birmingham. I said ok. She called workmen's comp and got it set up.

I got an appointment to see my neurosurgeon on April 7, which was the following week, and Dr Pitts on April 21. I'm trying to get in touch with my attorney now because I showed back up at work, clocked in and talked to the boss man. "Hey, driving the dump truck is all I have for you to do," he said.

"Well I have restrictions for no driving so let me get back with you," I told him.

"Okay, let the office manager know," he said, "and then get back with me."

That was on Wednesday. She said that she would call workmen's comp and let them know, so I told her to call me and let me know something. She said that she would call me but she never did. It's Thursday and I'm back at work again because I don't want them to say that I just quit. A quitter is one thing that I am not. I showed back up again and the same thing was said to me.

"If you can't drive a truck anymore," he told me, "then we don't have anything for you to do."

So I just waited on my check. My sister and her husband told me some things to ask my boss Chris, but my brain was too heavy at the time. I called her and the first thing she said was, "Did you ask him what we told you to?"

"No," I said. I wasn't thinking and just forgot.

"I'll be leaving my house in 15 minutes and I will meet you up there," she said. She showed up and started asking Chris and Cheryl questions at a mile a minute. The office manager was doing all the answering but what was getting to me was she was smiling so hard like this was a big joke or something. I'm a changed man since I almost lost my life, so me and my sister left and went outside.

"You need to call your attorney and let him know what's going on," she said.

"I been trying to call him, leaving him messages and haven't got a call back yet and it's been 3 days now," I said.

"Keep trying," she suggested. "And when you get him, call me on three-way."

I said ok. That was Thursday and I called him all that day as well as Friday with the same result. I left messages and still got nothing. I knew right then that I needed to find a workmen's comp attorney. But on Monday, I will try him again but what I was really hoping for was a workmen's comp attorney, I heard of one that specializes in criminal cases. I will try my old attorney again on Monday because he really needs to know what's going on.

I didn't feel like my job was treating me fair. I had been with this company for seven years and even though I can't drive the concrete mixer like they wanted me to, I can't help that. And even thought I didn't need a license for the driving job that they offered me, they were still treating me like I was a stranger.

I was making $16.75 an hour and they wanted to drop me down to $10.50 an hour. As long as I've been there, they could have done me much better than that. I'm going to try to reach my attorney again on Monday and just go from there.

Monday is here and my sister and I talked to my attorney and he felt the same way we did. I should be getting paid while I'm waiting the three weeks to go see Dr. Pitts. He also got me a test set up in Decatur called a vocational evaluation test, which is for workers' compensation injuries. He wanted to wait for my doctor's appointment on April 21 and then April 24.

I go and take the test that he had set up for me. It would all be done the same week and I'm so glad. My attorney will then determine what to do from there. At my appointment with Dr. Pitts, I let him know what was going on.

"My job wants me to drive a dump truck," I told him. "I don't need a license to drive it because it doesn't leave the yard, and my cleaning up has come to an end. They don't need anybody there cleaning, truck drivers only. I never got to drive the truck. But just riding in it for a couple hours every day was aggravating my injury."

He wrote out two prescriptions. One was for the pain and one was a muscle relaxer. Then he wrote me an excuse to return back to work with my same restrictions. I checked out and left.

The next morning I took my return back to work to my boss and I handed the doctor's excuse to him and he would not take it. "What is that?," he asked.

"My return back to work from my doctor," I said.

"We thought you quit," he told me.

"CHRIS, I've been here for seven years with this company. Why would I quit?"

He said, "Well, workmen's comp said anything else your doctor gives you, you need to give it to your attorney."

I left and went to the unemployment office and filled out for unemployment. I took care of that and now I'm getting ready to go see Mrs. Bramlett today, Friday April 24 at

1:30 for a vocational evaluation test. That's a test given to all workers' compensation injuries. The test was given in Decatur, Alabama. I'm here now with Mrs. Bramlett and she has everything- all my paperwork, my x-rays.

The test lasted for about three hours but it was all worth it. "I know you have heard this a lot," she said. "I'm just glad to see you here." She was blown away by my x-rays and how I had all that metal from my skull all the way down to c5 bone. I kind of felt like I was back in school with all the testing.

Before I walked out, she told me when she got all of my doctors' records, she would come up with a percentage for my being disabled—50 percent, 75 percent, 90 percent. She would be the person to determine that.

Back at home, I'm chilling and trying to stay focused. I can't do any work right now. I've filed for unemployment and by my last job lying to them and saying that I voluntarily quit, they turned me down. Sitting here with no money coming in, after working from a young age—I guess I was 14 years old when I got my first job—and worked all the way up to my accident, age 34. I'm a man who is used to working most of his life, always up to working and about to lose his life from working; it's not a good feeling at all.

I know the Lord didn't keep me here for nothing. I still have work to do. My job on this Earth is nowhere near being finished. So in the meanwhile, I'm just taking it easy until I find out what's going to be the deal with my situation.

CHAPTER EIGHT

My Disability & Ending Friendships

It's now July 2, 2009. I'm still waiting on something to go down with my case. I talked to Mrs. Bramlett again and she is still waiting on some more of my records. It seemed like Birmingham Hospital was the only one she was waiting on. So when they send the necessary paperwork, she will be able to make her determinations on my situation.

I applied for my disability and was turned down the first time and I applied again and was now just waiting to hear back from them. I cannot find work because of my restrictions. But I've still been looking. Not working, for me, is not good.

So now I'm just sitting here, still waiting on the verdict as to whether I'll ever be able to work again or not. And all of this idle time at home has made me very unhappy. I'm still here with the same lady that was with me throughout my accident and recovery.

My family was going to be there regardless. But I'm just beginning to feel like she thinks I owed her something for being there. I thank her for all the time she spent because she always brought it up whenever we had an argument. But just being real about this situation, if I was in her shoes and had five kids and the same thing happened to someone that I was close to, I wouldn't have put my kids off on my family or my friends. Family and friends weren't there when the children were conceived. Now I do love this woman but something is going on inside of her and the sad thing is that she knows what it is and don't care about fixing it.

People used to tell me about stress and I used to wonder what it felt like. Well I don't have to worry anymore because me and stress are like best friends now, and I am not happy at all about it and i want it out of my life. Stress can kill you if you let it.

I never thought that a woman with five kids would bring this on. I loved the children like a biological father loves his kids. As I got a little better, I just could not take any more stress from this woman. So I told her we just needed to be friends. She said that we could as long as she was under my roof. I said cool.

So now we are pretty much like roommates and I loved it this way- even though we still had our moments. I'm a single guy now getting ready to enjoy the rest of my life in peace. My friend and the kids will be moving out at the end of the month and I'm really looking forward to that.

She will be in her own place and I will still be here in mine. She told me that I could still see the children whenever I wanted to and I planned to do just that because they were really good kids and it's not their fault that we're not going to stay a couple.

My Momma told me a long time ago, "Son, you are a good man. Stop rushing into these relationships. Just let the Lord send you a good woman."

After hearing that over and over again from Momma, I said, "You are so right. I'm just going to chill and stay focused on what I've got going on. It's a new day. Thank God for waking me."

My homeboy Carl and I had some plans for later that night. He's like a big brother to me but he had some things going on. He had an old lady at home that I am so crazy about because she's always been like a sister to me and even though she's not too happy with me now, I will always love her like a sister.

Mrs. Keshia, if you decide to read this book, I just want you to know from the bottom of my heart I am SORRY.

Now back to my story, he also had a baby on the side that she knew about. I already knew his live-in girlfriend because we all grew up in Lincoln Projects. After my accident, he started coming to see me and then months later, he had a bad stroke.

Shan and I stuck with him throughout his stay at Huntsville Hospital. Later, they sent him to Lawrenceburg, Tenn. to another hospital that had therapy. When he had gotten better and got out, we started having fun again. We started bowling, fishing and going out to eat almost every day. We were spending crazy money. Even though we had five kids at home, we could afford it.

He was waiting on his disability to kick in. Whenever it did, he wouldn't owe me anything. To me, it's always the thought that counts. Once his money started coming in, our time was cut short. He started hanging around friends that weren't even there for him, but it was cool. I just stayed to myself, focusing on my book and my music.

During the time that we did hang, I got a chance to meet his new baby's mama TINA and she seemed to be pretty cool. Now his new baby's mama and the woman that he was staying with, had a falling out about something. I was the one taking him to spend time with his baby. But he had to visit undercover because if the woman he was staying with found out, their relationship would have come to an abrupt end.

His baby's mama Tina and I stayed cool even when I chose to not be around him because the old him was slowly beginning to rear its head. I really didn't like Carl's other side. Tina said that Carl always asked about me. So I decided to pop up one day and we started back hanging out.

One of his baby's mama's friends, Ree Ree, went to Calhoun College. She called and asked me if we wanted to go out to eat at Ruby Tuesdays. I asked him and he said yeah. We met them in the parking lot of a local motel and I drove. We left about eight and came back about 9:30. We had all loaded back up in my van. Tina, his baby's mama, the baby and her friend Ree Ree and I headed back to the motel to their ride. To our surprise, Shan and Keshia were waiting there for us.

They were outside fussing, cussing and crying. I understood Keshia being upset but not Shan because we weren't together even though we lived together. We hadn't been a couple in three months. I really didn't know why she was so upset. Calling my momma, telling her—like I'm going to get in trouble. Please. My momma and I are real close and I don't keep anything from her. Somebody brought them to the motel in the girl's car that he was staying with and they left when we pulled up.

Now they have to ride back with me and him. The two girls and his baby got out and the other two got in. Riding down the street, they're still arguing back and forth. He couldn't say much because the stroke took his voice. Now, it's funny because the only words he could say were all the bad ones.

He turned around and acted like he was going to hit her and Shan started acting crazy, opening the van door while I was driving, trying to get him to get out the van and I guess fight her or what ever.

I was on the phone with my momma at the time and she said I needed to be careful being around all that clowning. I dropped his girl Keshia off at her car and took him home.

Then Shan and I headed to my place. We made it in the house and she said, "Do you have a problem with me?"

"Yes," I answered. "You have not changed at all; you're still acting like you used to and I don't like it."

This was at 11o'clock at night and she woke the kids up. Full of anger, she told them to pack their stuff. And after everybody was packed and loaded up, she had me take them to a shelter for the homeless. They were far from homeless, but she wanted to go by choice. I took them like she asked and dropped them off.

The next day, she called and asked me to bring some stuff—clothes and food—to her friend's house. I told her to make sure somebody was there; she said there was. As I pulled up to the friend's house Shan came out the door, got the stuff, took it in and didn't say a word. Neither did I.

I left and went on about my way. She called me again the following day and said, "I need you to come pick me up from my friend's house and take me to your house. I need to get some stuff."

Continuing to play her game, I picked her up and two of the girls wanted to come, too. We made it and she started loading up stuff. I sat in my studio until they were ready to leave. When they were loaded up and said they were ready, I took them back and they unloaded the van.

I left and went back home. I walked in and checked everything out and man, I tell you, I don't know why they just didn't load up the whole house and put it in the van. They took all the food in the house, even took all the tissue, even the roll that had been used. I'm not mad; whatever she needed to leave, that was cool with me just as long as she was gone.

I'm at home now with no more stress. Maybe this stiffness that I've been feeling will ease away; I sure hope so.

CHAPTER NINE

My New Attorneys & Closing Case

It's July 14, 2009. I'm thanking God for laying me down and waking me up this morning. I'm getting back used to being at home alone again. It wasn't anything I wasn't used to. I'm going to keep it like this until I get married. I refuse to live with another woman unless we are married. Until then, it's all about patience. I've just about got my place back in order.

I'm at home with no food in the house. I talked to an old friend and she stocked me back up with groceries. Boy, ain't God good? Shan and those little babies will always be in my life because it's not their fault what's going on. I'm getting up, going for my walk like I do every morning except on Sundays; that's the Lord's day. Sunday is for church and resting up for a new week.

I'm still waiting on these cases to be done and over. I'm still waiting to hear from my worker's compensation case, my appeal with unemployment, and my disability case.

They've been gone now for almost two weeks. This will just be something I will have to get used to. But with me being a blessed young man, I'll get over it. What I was hoping is that we could still be friends out of all this. She's making it real hard by staying stuck in the past.

She texted me one day and asked could she and the babies use the van. I told her yes, but I had a lot to do this week, trying to make some money. We talked on Monday and she needed the van on Wednesday. I asked her did she know how long she would need it.

She said, "No, I don't but when I'm done, I will drop it back off wherever I pick it up from."

"It will be over my mother's house about 7 a.m. Wednesday morning," I told her.

"Okay," she said.

In the meanwhile, a friend asked me to do some work for her. Knowing that I had no money coming in, my family and friends looked out for me as much as they could and I thank them so much for that. I sent a text to Shan and asked her to call me. My phone finally rang after three hours and it was her. "Are you sure you don't know how long you'll be?," I asked her. "Because I need to make this money so I can pay my bills."

"Well, I don't want to inconvenience you so don't worry about it. I'll be fine," she said.

"Okay," I said.

Not long after that, she sent me a long text saying: "I thought you were going to have something to do. Anyway, thanks for trying. If there was any doubt in my mind that I made the wrong decision about leaving, you cleared it up because I was missing you and so were the kids. At this point, I see that it ain't anything and never was to you. That's my fault though for trying to give my all and trying to get someone to give the same."

She goes on to say, "From this point on we do not need to have anymore contact with each other" and she tells me that, "It's bad we are in this situation. All you have to worry about is bills."

I don't feel bad about this because I did not tell anyone to leave. She left by choice. Now, this is her third time leaving me and coming back. This time, I left it in God's hands. I'd like to say that everything happens for a reason. With this serious accident I had, it was just too much weight and stress. Something had to change and it did.

Even though she didn't like the situation, it was only for the best. Thank God because now we can move on with our lives and enjoy. Time is moving on and I'm dealing with my first cousin Emma in the hospital fighting cancer.

I went to visit her one day. She had a little mild surgery going on where they implanted a tube into her like an IV so they could give her medicine. I stayed about an hour and a half and went home because I had to be up early the next morning. I got up and went to handle my business and in the midst of it all, my phone rang and I was told that my cousin Emma had two days to two weeks to live. I wasn't looking for news like that but dealing with real life, it's known to happen.

That evening I went up there to see her and man, it didn't look good. I grabbed her hand and tried to talk to her but with that oxygen mask on, she couldn't really say anything. I was looking in her eyes and they were rolling back in her head. It didn't look good at all. Her blood pressure was so low; it was 58 over 34, I believe. I didn't stay long because I didn't want to keep looking at her like that.

On July 28, my little great-niece and I were watching TV. I called my sister Doris because she spent the night with her and I wanted to let her know that I had spoken with my attorney. I wanted to let her know what was said. I asked her how Emma was doing and she said since last night, she went down some more.

I got done talking to her and started back watching TV with my great-niece and less than one hour later, my phone rang again. It was my sister. Now for her to be calling me back that quick, I knew already what it was. I answered and just heard her talking; I knew it wasn't good.

On July 28 at around 10:30 a.m, Emma left us. We loved Emma but God loved her most. Remember what I said earlier? Now do you believe that death come in threes? Well if so, how did it end up as a total of four for me? Well I'll tell you why. *It's because death doesn't have a number*, and if God is ready for you, you're leaving. It doesn't matter if it's three, four or four hundred, when it's your time, you're going.

It's been one week now since we buried my dear cousin Emma and the family seemed to be doing ok, but this is something that we all will have to face one day. It might not be cancer. It could be something worse than that or something accidental like my situation. Only the Lord knows.

In the meanwhile, I'm still here dealing with the pressures of my life. I got a call from my attorney a couple days ago and he told me that workmen's comp had an offer on the table. And he wanted to know whether or not I would accept it. He told me to call him on Monday and let him know.

I hadn't been working and all my bills had jammed up on me. I wanted to go ahead and take it but at the same time, I wanted to make sure it's what I deserved for what I went through. For the rest of my life, it will be a health situation on and off that I will have to deal with.

My sister Doris and I had a meeting on Thursday, August 13, 2009 to talk with another attorney about my disability. They also dealt with workmen's comp cases too. So we will just put everything on the table Thursday morning at 10 a.m. It's the day of the meeting and everything went good with the new attorney.

She asked my sister if she was an attorney because she spoke like one. As we went over all of the paperwork, my sister had everything that I had- even my x-rays. This is the firm I'll be dealing with from now on: SINIARD, TIMBERLAKE & LEAGUE, P.C. My old attorney is now history.

My new attorneys do everything; they even got my disability on a roll. I have a telephone interview with the Social Security Administration on August 18 at 10 a.m. Now here's something strange to me- I would call my old attorney, leave him messages. Days would pass sometimes weeks and then just out the blue I would call one day, and he would be there.

Now, since the little money offer has come up, he's calling me. But I'm not going to take that offer and I never got to tell him that. Since they received my letter from my new attorneys, he's been calling me. He left me a voicemail message saying that the boss wanted him to talk to me. I didn't know what he wanted because I even called and left a message to call me, but they may have just been too busy to handle a case like mine. Thanks anyway.

I needed to ask my new attorney a question today so I called and she wasn't in. They sent me to her voicemail and I left her a message to call me. It was about 9 a.m. so I went on with my day and ended up at my mom's house. About 7 p.m., I'm sitting around talking to my sister on my mother's house phone and my cell phone rang; it was my attorney. I thought she would just call tomorrow since it was a little late, but she told me she had been tied up all day and was returning my phone call.

I said thanks and told her that I just wanted to ask her a couple of questions. We talked for a little while and she told me that I had three cases going on with them. I didn't know that. I thought it was just two, but besides the workman's comp and disability case, I also had another case called a third party disability case. That is where the concrete truck that I was driving is involved now, making it a third party.

We had a phone interview today with Mrs. Brown; she's a part of the new lawyer firm. It went pretty good, lasted about an hour and a half, but it was worth it. They had plenty of questions for me as far as my accident: all the doctors, all my medicine, all of the therapy, all the hospitals, just everything pertaining to my injury. My disability appeal is on the move. Thank God.

Tuesday, August 25, 2009, we had a meeting with another attorney. We talked about that third party case that he thinks I might have with the concrete truck. We talked about 30 minutes and he told me he was going to get on this case right now because if there's a case, it would have to be filed before September 19, 2009. The reason why is my accident would be at its two-year mark and my case wouldn't be worth anything. He told me to make an appointment to see him back one week before my two-year mark was up.

I will never forget what he told me before I left. "I've been doing attorney work like this for 30 years," he said, "and I have never had a case bad as yours. We have had some bad neck injuries that may have even had them paralyzed, and your injury was worse than theirs—and you're still up walking through all this."

His last words before we departed were, "It is very good to be working with a miracle man."

He shook my hand and said, "Take care, miracle man."

Monday morning August 31, I'm about to call my attorney's office and set my appointment. I'll also talk to them about some financial help. All my bills have piled up on me and I needed some help. I'm hoping they could help me out because here's the thing: if they could give me the money, they know they would get it back because when I get my settlement, the money goes to my attorney first.

Tuesday, September 9, I wanted to talk to my attorney about another possible law suit. I don't know but I talked to my attorney. I told her something that I forgot to bring up before: I had to have a double surgery because when Huntsville Hospital did the first surgery, there were broken bones and metal left in my incision when they stapled me up.

When they sent me to Birmingham, the doctor there saw that it had set up infection, which led me to have another surgery. She said that they could try but it would be hard because stuff like that could happen. So I told her what my sister Doris, my second mama, told me. She said that they did take care of me and saved my life so she wouldn't worry about another law suit.

"But Sis," I defended my actions, "I got to say something on that. God saved my life and the doctor was just the vessel that he used to save me through."

After I was about done talking to my attorney, I asked her about setting up an appointment with another attorney. "Ok," she said. "Hold on for a minute."

She came back to the phone and said she just talked to this attorney and he told her to tell me that far as that third case, it wasn't going to go because by what the police report was saying, the accident was my fault.

"I know you don't remember," she said.

"No, I don't," I told her. "But hey, we still have two cases that's pretty much a go."

"You're right," she said.

We told each other have a good day and departed.

CHAPTER TEN

GOD'S BLESSING

On September10, 2009, I'm sitting on the couch just taking it easy and I heard a horn blow outside. It was the mail lady with a certified letter from my attorney's office. I opened it up and it was about the third-party claim. When I read it, it said that the witnesses claimed that I ran a red light, hit another car and then flipped.

I understand what the witnesses are saying but the truck I was driving is not a fast one with no load. I had nine yards of cement on the truck. The extra weight would have made it that much slower. I was on Winchester Road. By what I was told, there was a Family Dollar store right there at that light on the corner, and I was told my tire marks started way before the store. I really don't remember any of this but I really don't know what made me put on brakes. This would have been just my third case with them. It's not going to go down, but I still have two cases that I know for sure are going to go down.

Sunday night chilling at my mom's house having dinner, my momma, my stepdad, my sister, her husband, my nephew and his girlfriend had all just made it back from their cruise the day before. Everybody's belly was full. My mom and I were sitting in the den watching TV. Everybody else was at the table talking and my accident popped up. I was just laying there listening because by me still being here through all of this, I'll probably be hearing this for the rest of my life. I ain't mad. I'm blessed.

Friday, October 8, 2009, I talked to Mrs. Bramlett's secretary, and she told me that Mrs. Bramlett had made her determination on my vocational disability rating. She rated it to be 100 percent. I'm headed back down my mom's house. I'm staying with her and the man I've been calling daddy for years. My mom had a knee replacement surgery so I'm staying with her until she gets better. That's Mommy, the love of my life.

Dr. Anderson is my care doctor now and he recommends that I have some more therapy set up because the stiffness in my neck was really bad. I'm back in now therapy three days a week. I have 12 visits with them. Each visit is for one hour and I have two visits left and I will be done. This time, I'll stay on it.

They told me for the rest of my life I'll need to do at least 30 to 45 minutes a day. That shouldn't be too bad. Even though they had worked with me in the past, they only worked with me by my symptoms or just how I told them I felt at the moment. I brought them my X-rays and they just could not believe I was there talking to them. What I had was a human decapitation.

Well world, my case is about over. My settlement is about done. I can go on living without the wonders and worries about how things will turn out. I shouldn't be worried anyway because GOD had my back, so whatever happens will be meant to happen because it will be through Him.

As far as getting up every morning and going to work to get a paycheck every week—that is probably done. Yes, my Lord has sent me two blessings. He has blessed me with my life and he has also blessed me financially as well. My truck driving career may be over, but I just like to thank God it's not my life. God bless you, and thank you for listening.

**These are the two men God put in my life to be a part of my blessing. Chad Tillman and Andrew Smith rescued me from my overturned truck.

Printed in the United States
By Bookmasters